Adorable Furniture
for
Dolls & Teddy Bears

ADORABLE FURNITURE
FOR
DOLLS & TEDDY BEARS

Anita Louise Crane

Sterling Publishing Co, Inc., New York
A Sterling/Chapelle Book

Chapelle Ltd.

Owner: Jo Packham

Editor: Linda Orton

Staff: Marie Barber, Ann Bear, Areta Bingham,
Kass Burchett, Rebecca Christensen, Marilyn Goff,
Holly Hollingsworth, Susan Jorgensen,
Barbara Milburn, Karmen Quinney, Leslie Ridenour,
Cindy Stoeckl, Gina Swapp

Photography: Kevin Dilley, photographer for
Hazen Photography

Pfaff American Sales Corporation
P.O. Box 566
Paramus, NJ 07653-0566
A special thanks for the sewing machine used in
slipcover projects.

Library of Congress Cataloging-in-Publication

Crane, Anita Louise
    Adorable furniture for dolls & teddy bears / Anita Louise Crane.
      p. cm.
    Includes index.
    "A Sterling/Chapelle Book."
    ISBN 0-8069-4493-5
    1. Doll furniture. I. Title.

TT175.5 .C73 2000
745.592'3--dc21   00-028511

10 9 8 7 6 5 4 3 2 1

A Sterling/Chapelle Book

Published by Sterling Publishing Company, Inc.
387 Park Avenue South, New York, NY 10016
© 2000 by Anita Louise Crane
Distributed in Canada by Sterling Publishing
% Canadian Manda Group, One Atlantic Avenue, Suite 105
Toronto, Ontario, Canada M6K 3E7
Distributed in Great Britain and Europe by Cassell PLC
Wellington House, 125 Strand, London WC2R 0BB, England
Distributed in Australia by Capricorn Link (Australia) Pty Ltd.
P.O. Box 6651, Baulkham Hills, Business Centre, NSW 2153, Australia
Printed in China
All Rights Reserved

Sterling ISBN 0-8069-4493-5

Plaid Enterprises, Inc.
P.O. Box 117600
Norcross, GA 30091-7600
Phone: (770) 923-8200
A special thanks for the paints and
finishes used on wood furniture projects.

Walnut Hollow
1409 State Road 23
Dodgeville, WI 53533
Phone: (800) 950-5101
A special thanks for the furniture and
trims used in wood furniture projects.

The written instructions, designs, photographs, patterns, and projects in this volume are intended for the personal use of the reader and may be reproduced for that purpose only. Any other use, especially commercial use, is forbidden under law without the written permission of the copyright holder.

Every effort has been made to ensure that all of the information in this book is accurate. However, due to differing conditions, tools, and individual skills, the publisher cannot be responsible for any injuries, losses, and/or other damages which may result from the use of the information in this book.

Due to the limited amount of space available, we must print our patterns at a reduced size in order to give our patrons the maximum number of projects possible in our publications. We believe the quality and quantity of our patterns will compensate for any inconvenience this may cause.

If you have any questions or comments, please contact:

Chapelle Ltd., Inc.
P.O. Box 9252
Ogden, UT 84409

Phone: (801) 621-2777
FAX: (801) 621-2788
e-mail: chapelle@chapelleltd.com
website: www.chapelleltd.com

Anita Louise Crane has been designing, creating, photographing, painting, writing, and marketing since 1981. She is best known for her one-of-a-kind teddy bears.

She has been a special-occasion and wedding dress designer and seamstress, as well as proprietress of the Bearlace Cottage in Park City, Utah.

Anita currently runs her teddy bear business by appointment from her home. She specializes in her watercolor paintings and creation of teddy bears, bunnies, and mice. She has a wonderful collection of vintage laces and linens. Anita is spending a significant amount of time these days in the creation of her craft project books, as well as illustrating and writing a child's book, which is the dream of her life.

She is the author of *Teddy Bear Magic, Two-Hour Teddy Bears, Two-Hour Dolls' Clothes,* and *Making Adorable Teddy Bears.*

Anita resides in Park City, Utah, with her husband Bruce and kitty Raisen. She is the mother of four and grandmother of nine. She is usually busy stitching up slipcovers and creating decorative projects for her home. She spends the remainder of her time painting and enjoying the mountains.

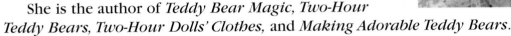

For Jennifer, Rachael, Gabriella, Whitney, Holly, Jeannie, and all the other "little girls" in my life.

A special thank-you to Peg Ross for her lovely log cabin quilt and pattern on pages 120–121.

A thank-you to my editor, Linda Orton, for her thorough checking and rechecking of all the instructions I submit. Linda, I couldn't do it without you. It is such a pleasure working with you on each book.

Table of Contents

Introduction

The furniture in *Adorable Furniture for Dolls & Teddy Bears* is made from readily available materials and objects such as boxes and unfinished doll furniture. Learn to personalize doll furniture with découpage, wood trims, and paint ideas.

Make a table using a commercial cutting board and curtain rod finials. Style an overstuffed chair with a pretty floral slipcover, cardboard box, and quilt batting. A turned chair leg is perfect for a floor lamp and a wooden serving tray will make a splendid bed for your favorite doll or stuffed animal.

Once you begin to make these delightful doll furniture pieces, you will enjoy the effort of creation and the accomplishment of completed, attractive, and completely functional doll furniture.

The furniture projects have been divided by rooms, but you do not have to feel limited since many will be perfect for other rooms or as an accent to collectable dolls.

General Instructions

Work Area

It is best to have a dedicated workspace with a table and floor that is protected or unaffected by any spills. Old newspapers to protect and clean rags to wipe up spills will help keep your workspace clean. Discarded margarine containers and glass jars with lids are perfect for mixing and saving paints.

It is critical to use nontoxic water-based paints when creating furniture that will be used by children. All paints used in *Adorable Furniture for Dolls & Teddy Bears* projects are water-based, nontoxic, and can be cleaned up with soap and water.

The following equipment and materials will come in handy for assembling projects:

Craft scissors
Drill with drill bits
Duct tape
Hot-glue gun and glue sticks
Paintbrushes:
    detail: #8; #6
    flat: ½"; 1"
Screwdriver
Staple gun with staples
Tape measure
Wood glue

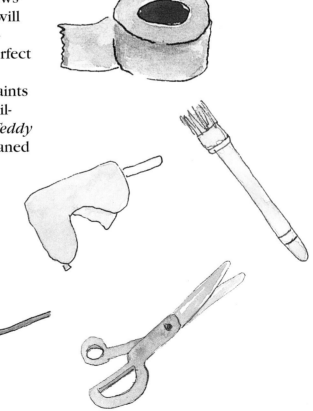

The following items are helpful for any projects that require stitching:
Fabric scissors
Pins:
 ball-head
 straight
 T-pins
Sewing machine
Sewing needles
Sewing thread

Découpage

Materials:
Découpage medium
Art such as: color copies, greeting
 cards, tissue, or pictures from books

Equipment:
Craft scissors
Paintbrushes: ½" or 1" (size is dependent
 on the size of art)
Stencil brush: (very helpful with art from
 greeting cards or card stock)

Instructions:

Step 1
a. Cut out art.

Step 2
a. Brush light coat of découpage medium
on back of art.

b. Place art on furniture and
smooth out with fingers,
making certain that all
air bubbles are removed.
*Note: Use stencil brush to tap on
card stock, so it will adhere better
to the surface and remove air
bubbles.* Allow to dry.

Step 3
a. Brush découpage medium over art, slightly overlapping edges. Allow to dry 20–30 minutes.

b. Apply second coat and allow to dry. *Note: Repeated coats will give a filled-in finish and the appearance of having been hand-painted.*

c. After final coat of découpage medium is completely dry, apply varnish to seal the artwork and furniture.

Paintbrushes

Paintbrushes are sold individually or may be purchased in packaged sets. The project equipment lists in this book will call for a ½" or 1" flat paintbrush, or #6 or #8 detail brush. Some instructions will call for a combination.

The flat paintbrushes are used to cover large flat areas with paint, découpage, or varnish. Use the 1" on tabletops, chair seats, or anywhere the surface to be painted is larger than the paintbrush. The ½" paintbrush can be used on chair and table legs, slats, or surfaces between ½" and 1".

Detail brushes are used to paint in small areas such as the crevices in wooden trims or decorative elements of stripes, dots, flowers, or other small details.

Stitches

Gather Stitch
Machine-stitch or hand-stitch
two parallel rows of stitches.
Pull thread ends to gather
fabric.

Overcast Stitch
Connect two sections by
hand-stitching back and forth
through one section and then
the other.

Cording

Cording is used as a decorative element on upholstered furniture.

Materials:
Cording
Fabric
Sewing thread

Equipment:
Sewing machine with zipper foot

Instructions:

Step 1
a. Cut cording to desired length.

b. Cut or tear 1½" strip of fabric same length as cording.

Step 2

a. Place cording in center of strip on wrong side of fabric.

b. Fold fabric over cord and stitch along edge of cording as shown in Illustration A.

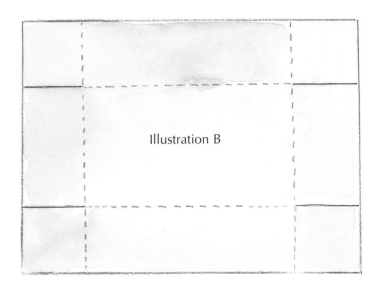

Illustration A

Tip: Pin and/or stitch cording to one piece of fabric to keep cording from slipping when sandwiching cording between two pieces of fabric.

Making Boxes

The boxes used in the upholstered furniture pieces are standard sizes and should be available from any shipping store.

If a box is unavailable or you prefer to make your own from cardboard, the following instructions will be useful.

Materials:
Cardboard
Duct tape

Equipment:
Pencil
Tape measure
Utility knife

Instructions:

Step 1
a. Use the following formula to determine the size of your finished box:

(2 x height) + length = length of cardboard
(2 x height) + width = width of cardboard

Note: Additional length and width will need to be figured in if making a box with flaps or lid.

b. Mark the height on all four sides of cardboard with dotted lines for folding and solid lines for cutting as shown in Illustration B .

Illustration B

Step 2
a. Cut box along solid lines.

b. Score and fold box on dotted lines. Tape box to secure.

Adorable
Furniture for the Living Room

PLAID Sofa

Sofa Frame

Materials:
Cardboard: 2' x 3'
Cardboard box with closing flaps:
    11"w x 2½"h x 17"l
Duct tape
Empty paper towel rolls: (2)
Quilt batting: twin size
Sewing thread
Spray adhesive
Wood glue
Wooden ball knobs: 2½" (4)

Equipment:
Hammer
Heavy-duty scissors or utility knife
Roofing nails: (4)
Sewing needle
Staple gun with staples
Tape measure

Instructions:

Note: See General Instructions for Making Boxes on page 11.

Step 1

a. Glue one knob onto each corner on bottom of box.

b. Using hammer and nails, secure knobs to box from inside as shown in Illustration A.

c. Securely tape box flaps closed.

Illustration A

13

Step 2

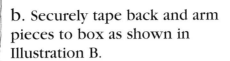

a. Cut one 8½" x 17" piece for back and two 8½" x 11" pieces for arms from cardboard.

b. Securely tape back and arm pieces to box as shown in Illustration B.

c. Securely tape one towel roll to each arm as shown in Illustration C.

Illustration B

d. Fill inside of towel rolls with batting, allowing a small portion of batting to extend beyond tube ends.

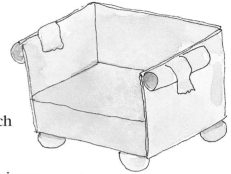

Illustration C

Step 3

a. Cut two pieces each from batting to cover front bottom, arms, and both sides of back.

b. Using spray adhesive, spray one section and press batting over adhesive as shown in Illustration D. Repeat for each section. Repeat with second piece of batting for each section.

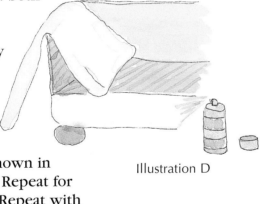

Illustration D

c. See General Instructions for Stitches on page 10. Using needle and thread, stitch ends of arms and front together with large overcast stitch as shown in Illustration E.

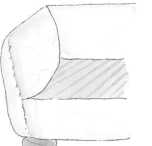

Illustration E

Sofa Cover

Materials:
Duct tape
Fabric: plaid, 2 yds.
Fabric glue
Fringe trim: heavy, 2 yds.
Polyester stuffing
Sewing thread

Equipment:
Fabric marking pencil
Fabric scissors
Hot-glue gun and glue sticks
Iron and ironing board
Pins:
    ball-head
    T-pins
Sewing machine
Sewing needle
Staple gun and staples

Instructions:

Step 1

a. Cut two 12" x 13" rectangles for outside arm and two 1½" x 13" rectangles for inside arm from fabric.

b. Using sewing machine and leaving ½" seam allowance, stitch one outside and one inside piece with right sides together along one long edge as shown in Illustration F.

c. Drape fabric, right side out, over arm. Repeat for remaining arm pieces.

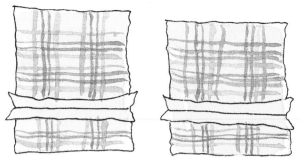

Illustration F

Step 2

a. Cut one 10½" x 19" rectangle for back and one 7½" x 19" rectangle for front section of back.

b. Stitch pieces with right sides together along one long edge as shown in Illustration G.

c. Drape fabric, right side out, over back.

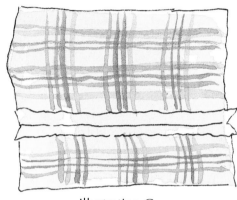

Illustration G

Illustration H

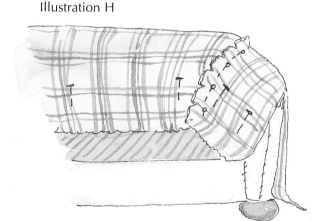

Step 3

a. Using T-pins, fit and secure draped pieces in place.

b. Match seams on inside. Using ball-head pins, tightly pin seams together as shown in Illustration H. Cut notches as necessary to allow for curve.

c. Match outside back and arm seams. Tightly pin together as shown in Illustration I.

d. Trim excess fabric, leaving ¾" seam allowance. Cut notches into seam for matching. Remove cover from sofa. Remove pins and place fabric with right sides together, matching notches. Stitch pieces together.

e. Turn cover right side out and place on sofa. Adjust any seams as necessary.

Illustration I

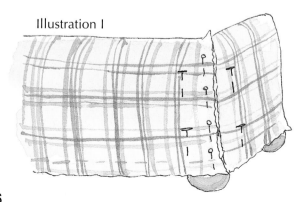

16

Step 4

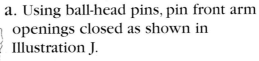

a. Using ball-head pins, pin front arm openings closed as shown in Illustration J.

b. Follow instructions for Step 3d.

c. Remove cover from sofa and turn inside out. Measure 1½" across and down from corner and mark as shown in Illustration K.

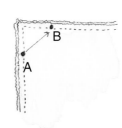

Illustration K

d. Press seam open. Match "A" to "B" in Illustration K and stitch as shown in Illustration L.

e. Cut top section leaving ½" seam allowance as shown in Illustration M.

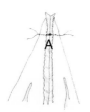

Illustration L

f. Follow instructions for Step 3e.

g. Staple raw edges in place as shown in Illustration N.

h. Using duct tape, cover staples and raw edges.

Illustration M

Illustration J

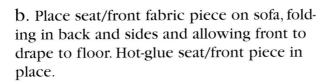

Illustration N

Step 5

a. Cut one 14½" x 17" rectangle for seat/front. Set aside.

b. Place seat/front fabric piece on sofa, folding in back and sides and allowing front to drape to floor. Hot-glue seat/front piece in place.

c. Using needle and thread, overcast-stitch arm front and seat/front together as shown in Illustration O.

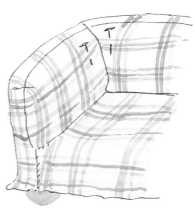

Illustration O

Step 6

a. Turn sofa over and hot-glue raw edges of cover onto cardboard as shown in Illustration P.

b. Turn chair right side up and hot-glue fringe trim onto bottom of sofa as shown in Illustration Q.

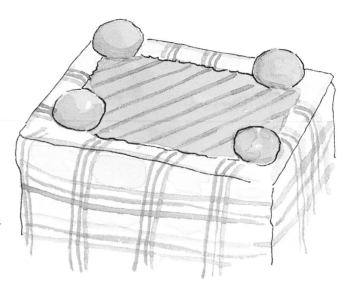

Illustration P

Illustration Q

Step 7

a. Cut one 17" x 23" piece of fabric for cushion. Fold fabric in half lengthwise with right sides together and stitch on two sides with ½" seam allowance.

b. Lightly fill open end with stuffing. Fold ends in and stitch closed.

Heart and Lace Table

Heart and Lace Table

Materials:
Acrylic paint: lt. green
Braid trim: ½"-wide, 1 yd.
Découpage medium
Gesso: white
Lace: 5"-wide, 1 yd.
Nontoxic varnish: gloss
Tissue napkin:
   rose-patterned
Wooden heart stool:
   9"w x 9"h x 9"l

Equipment:
Craft scissors
Hot-glue gun and
   glue sticks
Paintbrushes:
   flat: ½"; 1"
Pencil

Instructions:

Step 1

a. Mix equal amounts of gesso and lt. green paint. See General Instructions for Paintbrushes on page 10. Paint stool with gesso and paint mixture. Allow to dry.

b. Paint stool with lt. green. Allow to dry.

Step 2

a. Spread napkin on work surface and place stool with heart side down over rose napkin. Trace around heart shape.

b. Cut out heart shape. Discard second ply from napkin, retaining piece with rose pattern.

c. See General Instructions for Découpage on page 10. Découpage tissue onto tabletop as shown in Illustration A. *Note: Gently smooth and flatten, taking care not to tear napkin.* Allow to dry. *Note: If bubbles appear, prick them with a pin and gently pat down.*

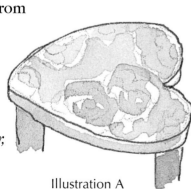

Illustration A

Step 3

a. Paint table with varnish. Allow to dry.

Step 4

a. Hot-glue lace around heart edge.

b. Hot-glue braid over top edge of lace as shown in Illustration B.

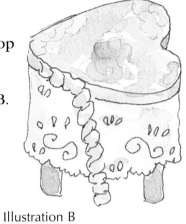

Illustration B

Variations:

- Découpage or paint stripes and polka dots on tabletop or table legs.

- Hot-glue tassels around edge of table.

- Hot-glue fringe around edge of table.

Country Table Lamp

Lamp Base

Materials:
Acrylic paints: black; leaf green;
    lt. pink; salmon; turquoise;
    red violet
Gesso: white
Nontoxic varnish: gloss
Wood glue
Wooden ball knob: 1½"
Wooden candlestick: 6¾"
Wooden spools: (2)

Equipment:
Paintbrushes:
    detail: #6
    flat: ½"; 1"

Instructions:

Step 1
a. Glue spools onto top of candlestick. Allow to dry.

b. Glue knob onto top of spools. Allow to dry.

Step 2
a. See General Instructions for Paintbrushes on page 10. Paint lamp with gesso. Allow to dry.

c. Paint lamp base sections as shown in Illustration A on page 24. Allow to dry between colors.

d. Paint stripes and dots on painted sections. Allow to dry.

e. Paint lamp with varnish. Allow to dry.

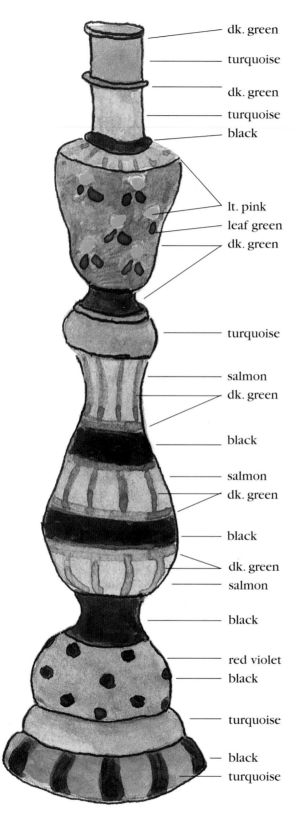

dk. green

turquoise

dk. green

turquoise

black

lt. pink

leaf green

dk. green

turquoise

salmon

dk. green

black

salmon

dk. green

black

dk. green

salmon

black

red violet

black

turquoise

black

turquoise

Illustration A

Lampshade

Materials:
Braid trim: ½"-wide, 14"
Fabric: cotton polka-dot, 24" x 4"
Lampshade: 3"w x 4"h x 5"d
Ribbon: plaid, 1¼"-wide, 24"
Thread

Equipment:
Hot-glue gun and glue sticks
Sewing machine
Sewing needle (optional)
Tape measure

Instructions:

Step 1
a. Using sewing machine, stitch ribbon 1" above one long edge of fabric.

b. See General Instructions for Stitches on page 10. Using sewing machine, gather-stitch two rows on opposite long edge of fabric. Gather fabric to fit top of lampshade plus ½".

c. Place short edges with right sides together and stitch with ¼" seam.

Step 2
a. Hot-glue gathered edge of fabric onto lampshade. *Optional: Using needle and thread, stitch fabric to lampshade.*

b. Hot-glue braid onto gathered edge of fabric.

Wingback Chair

Wingback Chair

Wingback Chair Frame

Materials:
Cardboard: 20" x 20"
Cardboard box with closing flaps:
   8"w x 4¾"h x 11¾"l
Duct tape
Empty toilet tissue rolls (2)
Newspaper
Quilt batting: high-loft, twin size
Sewing thread
Spray adhesive

Equipment:
Fabric scissors
Heavy-duty scissors or utility knife
Pencil
Sewing needle
Tape measure

Instructions:

Note: See General Instructions for Making Boxes on page 11.

Step 1

a. Push flaps to inside of box on one end. Securely tape flaps closed on other end.

b. Cut one 19¾" x 16¾" piece for back and wings from cardboard. Cut two 8" x 9¼" pieces for arms.

c. Trim and round upper corners of back and wings as shown in Illustration A.

d. Place back and wings on newspaper and trace separately, adding 1" all around to make pattern. Set aside for Step 4.

e. Mark and score wings 4" in from edges as shown by dotted lines in Illustration A.

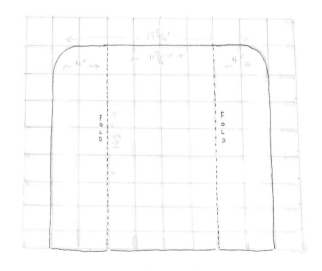

Illustration A

26

Step 2

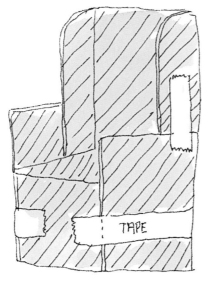

a. Securely tape back and wings to box as shown in Illustration B.

b. Securely tape arm pieces to box as shown in Illustration B.

c. Securely tape one tissue roll to each arm as shown in Illustration C.

d. Fill inside of tissue rolls with batting, allowing a small portion of batting to extend beyond tube ends.

Illustration B

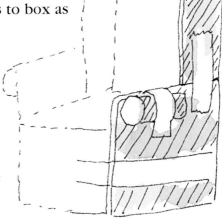

Illustration C

Step 3

a. Enlarge Arm Front Pattern on page 72 and Arm Pattern on page 73 200% and photocopy. Cut out patterns.

Step 4

a. Cut batting double the lengths of the sides and back patterns. Cut batting double the width of the wings. Set patterns aside for Wingback Chair Slipcover Instructions.

b. Using spray adhesive, spray one section and press batting over adhesive. Repeat for each section as shown in Illustration D. Trim excess batting. *Note: If more loft is desired, a second piece of batting may be cut and applied over first layer of batting.*

Illustration D

c. See General Instructions for Stitches on page 10. Using needle and thread, stitch ends of arms and front together with large overcast stitch. Stitch back and sides together as shown in Illustration E. *Notes: Extra batting may be added to areas that may need more rounding. The slipcover will compress the batting when it is placed on chair.*

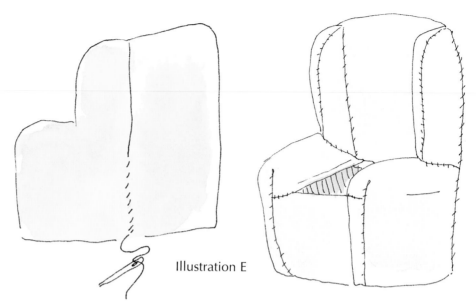

Illustration E

Wingback Chair Slipcover

Materials:
Cording: 2 yds. (optional)
Fabric: cotton, 3 yds.
Polyester stuffing
Sewing thread

Equipment:
Fabric marking pen
Fabric scissors
Hot-glue gun and glue sticks
Iron and ironing board
Masking tape
Pins:
    ball-head
    straight
    T-pins
Sewing machine
Sewing needle
Staple gun with staples
Tape measure

Instructions:

Step 1

a. Using straight pins, pin photocopied patterns from Wingback Chair Frame Instructions Steps 3 and 4a on page 27 to fabric and cut out.

b. Cut two pieces each for wings and chair back from patterns.

c. Cut one 11¼" x 13½" rectangle for seat/front of chair.

d. Cut three 5½" x 31" rectangles for chair ruffle.

e. Cut two 7½" x 11" rectangles for cushion.

Step 2

a. Drape chair Front/Back pieces, right side up, over chair.

b. Match seams on inside. Using ball-head pins, pin pieces together for a snug fit as shown in Illustration F.

c. Drape Wing pieces, right side up, over chair.

d. Match seams on inside. Using ball-head pins, pin pieces together for a snug fit as shown in Illustration F.

e. Trim excess fabric, leaving ¾" seam allowance. Cut notches every 2" to allow for curve and matching. Remove cover from chair.

f. *Optional: See General Instructions for Cording on page 11. Measure top and front edge of each wing. Cut 2"-wide strip of fabric and cording 1" longer than measurement. Tip: Contrasting fabric may be used for cording.*

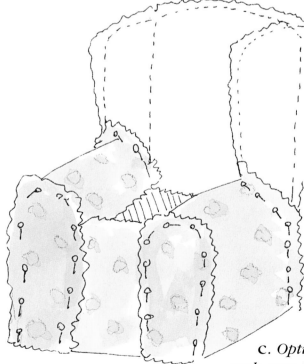

Illustration F

g. *Sandwich and pin cording between wing pieces with raw edges out. Notch cording to match wing pieces.*

h. Remove pins and place fabric with right sides together, matching notches. Using sewing machine, stitch pieces together.

i. Turn cover right side out and place on chair. Adjust any seams as necessary.

Step 3

a. Drape Arm piece over chair arm. Match Arm piece to Front/Back piece. Pin inside arm seam together as shown in Illustration G.

b. Trim excess fabric, leaving ¾" seam allowance. Cut notches every 2" to allow for curve and matching.

c. *Optional: Follow Steps 2f and 2g for top and front edge of each arm front.*

Illustration G

d. Mark on fabric where stitching will begin and end. Remove cover from chair. Remove pins and place fabric with right sides together, matching notches. Stitch pieces together.

e. Stitch running stitch across top of arm as indicated on Arm Pattern.

Step 4

a. Turn cover right side out and place on chair. Line up dots on Arm piece with dots on Arm Front piece.

b. Pin seam together, pulling on running stitch thread to ease fabric curve in place as shown in Illustration J on page 77.

c. Trim excess fabric, leaving ¾" seam allowance. Cut notches as necessary to allow for curve and matching.

d. Remove cover from chair. Remove pins and place fabric with right sides together, matching notches. Stitch pieces together.

Step 5

a. Place cover on chair and check fit. Add stuffing to fill out areas or make adjustments as needed.

b. Staple or tape raw fabric edges to box as shown in Illustration K on page 78.

Step 6

a. Fold under ½" on one long edge side of seat/front piece and press.

b. Place folded edge onto back of seat. Fold side edges under to fit shape of seat.

c. Hot-glue seat section in place, allowing front edge to loosely hang down.

d. See General Instructions for Stitches on page 10. Using needle and thread, overcast-stitch Arm and seat/front together.

e. Turn bottom raw edges of fabric inside box and hot-glue in place.

Step 7

a. Using sewing machine, stitch chair ruffle pieces together with ½" seam allowance to make one long strip.

b. Stitch ½" hem on each long side of ruffle.

c. Gather-stitch two rows on one long raw edge of ruffle. Gather ruffle to fit around chair.

d. Hot-glue ruffle around bottom edge of chair.

Step 8

a. Stitch three sides of cushion pieces with right sides together and ½" seam allowance. Turn right side out.

b. Fill cushion with stuffing. Fold ends in and stitch closed.

Lace Drape

Instructions:

Materials:
Ribbon or lace: scraps
Round lace doilies: (3)

*Note: Doilie size will be
determined by shelf or
mantle size.*

Step 1
a. Drape one doilie in center of shelf or mantle.

b. Drape remaining doilies on ends of shelf or mantle,
allowing them to overlap slightly.

Step 2
a. Gather overlapping edges of outside doilies and secure
with ribbon or lace.

b. Gather outside edge of each doilie and secure with
ribbon or lace.

Flower Wreath

Materials:
Dried berries
Dried or silk flowers: small
Dried leaves
Foam wreath base: small
Moss
Ribbon: 18"

Equipment:
Hot-glue gun and glue sticks

Instructions:

Step 1
a. Tie ribbon loop around top of wreath for hanging.
Note: Ribbon will not be seen in completed wreath.

Step 2
a. Hot-glue tufts of moss onto wreath until wreath is completely covered.

Step 3
a. Arrange dried flowers, leaves, and berries as desired on wreath.

b. Hot-glue flowers, leaves, and berries in place.

Adorable
Furniture for the Kitchen

TWIG TABLE

Materials:
Acrylic paint: red
Gesso: white
Nontoxic varnish: gloss
Twigs: ½"-dia.
Wood glue
Wooden doll table: 6"w x 6½"h x 6"l

Equipment:
Paintbrush:
 flat: 1"
Pencil
Rose clippers or wire cutters

Instructions:

Step 1

a. Mix equal amounts of gesso and red paint. Paint table with gesso and paint mixture. Allow to dry.

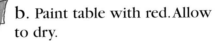

b. Paint table with red. Allow to dry.

c. Paint table with varnish. Allow to dry.

Step 2

a. Cut twigs into seventy-five 4" pieces.

b. Glue twigs onto one side of table as shown in Illustration A. Allow to dry. Repeat for remaining sides.

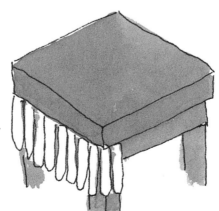

Illustration A

TWIG HUTCH

Materials:

Acrylic paint: red
Artificial fruit
Dried flowers
Moss (optional)
Mushroom birds: large (3–4)
Nontoxic varnish: gloss
Pinecones: small
Twigs
Wooden unfinished doll hutch:
    11"w x 20"h x 5¼"l

Equipment:

Hot-glue gun and glue sticks
Paintbrush:
    flat: 1"
Rose clippers or wire cutters

Instructions:

Step 1

a. Mix equal amounts of gesso and red paint. Paint table with gesso and paint mixture. Allow to dry.

b. Paint hutch with red. Allow to dry.

c. Paint hutch with varnish. Allow to dry.

Step 2

a. Cut twigs to cover upper front edge of hutch. Cut twigs in varying lengths to cover sides of hutch as shown in photograph on facing page.

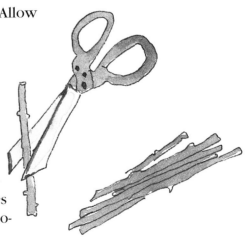

Illustration A

b. Lay hutch on its side and hot-glue twigs onto side of hutch as shown in Illustration A. Allow to cool.

c. Lay hutch on twig side and hot-glue twigs onto opposite side of hutch. Allow to cool.

d. Lay hutch on its back and hot-glue twigs onto upper front of hutch. Allow to cool.

Step 3

a. Hot-glue pinecones *and moss (optional)* onto top and sides of hutch.

b. Hot-glue fruit and dried flowers onto hutch as desired.

c. Hot-glue birds onto hutch as desired.

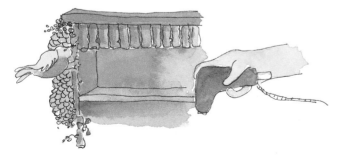

Carrot Chair

Carrot Chair

Materials:
Acrylic paints: metallic gold; lt. green
Art: color copy or greeting card
Découpage medium
Fringe: 3"-wide, gold (22")
Nontoxic varnish: gloss
Plastic carrots: 3" (2)
Wooden doll chair: 6¾"w x 15"h x 6¾"l

Equipment:
Craft scissors
Hot-glue gun and glue sticks
Paintbrushes:
   detail: #6
   flat: 1"

Instructions:

Step 1
a. See General Instructions for Paintbrushes on page 10. Paint chair with green. Allow to dry.

Step 2
a. Color copy Mother Bear Art on opposite page or use greeting card. Cut out art.

b. See General Instructions for Découpage on page 10. Découpage color copy onto chair back as shown in Illustration A. Allow to dry.

Illustration A

Step 3
a. Outline around art with metallic gold. Allow to dry.

b. Paint squiggly lines on legs and back of chair as shown in photograph on page 39. Allow to dry.

c. Paint a thin coat across back slats with gold, allowing green to show through. Allow to dry.

Mother Bear Art

Step 4

a. Paint chair with varnish. Allow
to dry.

Step 5

a. Hot-glue carrots onto chair back as
   shown in photograph at
   right.

b. Hot-glue fringe around
   edge of seat as shown
   in Illustration B.

Illustration B

Cat Cubby

Materials:
Acrylic paints: antique gold; lt. leaf
    green; med. green; dk. pink; red
    violet; yellow
Art: color copies or decals (3)
Braid trim: 1"-wide, ¾ yd.
Découpage medium
Fabric glue
Gesso: white
Masking tape: ½"-wide
Nontoxic varnish: gloss
Wood glue
Wooden ball knobs: 1½" (4)
Wooden cutout cats: 4½" (2)
Wooden doll cubby:
    10¼"w x 10½"h x 5"l
Wooden trim: 5⅜" x 1⅛"

Equipment:
Craft scissors
Paintbrushes:
    detail: #8
    flat: ½"; 1"
Pencil

Instructions:

Step 1

a. Using wood glue, glue trim onto bottom of cubby. Allow to dry.

b. Adhere flat side of knobs onto bottom of cubby legs. Allow to dry.

c. Adhere cats onto top of cubby. Allow to dry. *Optional: Angels, stars, or other wood cutouts may be used in place of cats.*

Step 2

a. See General Instructions for Paintbrushes on page 10. Paint cubby with gesso. Allow to dry.

b. Paint cubby with lt. leaf green. Allow to dry.

c. Paint ball-feet and knobs with med. green. Allow to dry.

Step 3

a. Apply masking tape in vertical strips, allowing ½" between strips on doors.

b. Paint untaped areas of door with antique gold. Allow to dry.

c. Remove tape.

Step 4

a. Paint small dots with dk. pink on doors over green stripes, ball-feet, and top of cubby. Allow to dry.

b. Randomly paint dots with red violet over dk. pink dots.

c. Paint leaves with med. green on red violet dots for flowers as shown in Illustration A.

Step 5

a. Paint horizontal stripes with yellow on cats, beginning halfway down the head.

b. Paint dots with yellow and leaves with med. green on upper section of cat's head and sides of cubby. Allow to dry.

Illustration A

Flowering Vine Art

Step 6

a. Color copy three Flowering Vine Art above at desired sizes. Cut out art or use decals.

b. See General Instructions for Découpage on page 10. Découpage one color copy onto top of cubby. Allow to dry.

c. Découpage one color copy onto each door. Allow to dry.

d. Paint swirls around outside edges of art as shown in Illustration B. Allow to dry.

Step 7

a. Paint cubby with varnish. Allow to dry.

b. Using fabric glue, glue fringe around outside edge of cubby.

Illustration B

Alternate Instructions for Cat Cubby on pages 41–43:

Materials:
Acrylic paints: black; blue; red; yellow
Gesso: white
Masking tape: ½"-wide
Nontoxic varnish: gloss
Wood glue
Wooden ball knobs: 1½" (4)
Wooden doll cubby:
    10¼"w x 10½"h x 5"l
Wooden star cutout
Wooden trims:
    5⅜" x 1⅛"
    corners: 3⅛" x 2⅜" (2)

Equipment:
Craft scissors
Paintbrushes:
    detail: #8
    flat: ½"; 1"
Pencil

Alternate Instructions:

Step 1

a. Glue 5⅜" x 1⅛" trim onto bottom of cubby. Allow to dry.

b. Adhere corner trims onto upper outside corner of each door. Allow to dry.

c. Adhere flat side of knobs onto bottom of cubby legs. Allow to dry.

d. Adhere stars onto upper inside corner of each door. Allow to dry.

Step 2

a. See General Instructions for Paintbrushes on page 10. Paint cubby with gesso. Allow to dry.

b. Paint cubby top, legs, and front edges with blue. Allow to dry.

c. Paint cubby doors, sides, and bottom trim with red. Allow to dry.

d. Paint cubby top edge, bottom front, and ball feet with yellow. Allow to dry.

Step 3

a. Apply masking tape in vertical strips on top edge, bottom front, and ball feet, allowing ½" between strips.

b. Paint untaped areas with black. Allow to dry.

c. Remove tape.

d. Paint stars with black. Allow to dry.

e. Paint polka dots on doors with black. Allow to dry.

Step 4

a. Paint cubby with varnish. Allow to dry.

Straw Hats

Materials:
Berries or silk flowers
Ribbon
Straw hat: small

Equipment:
Hot-glue gun and glue sticks

Instructions:

Step 1
a. Hot-glue ribbon around crown
of hat.

Step 2
a. Hot-glue berries or silk flowers
onto brim and crown of hat.

Variation #1:

• Velvet ribbon is hot-glued around crown of hat and several small bows and berries are hot-glued to ribbon and brim.

Variation #2:

• Polka-dot ribbon with two or more ribbon streamers are hot-glued around crown of hat and a variety of flowers are hot-glued onto one side.

Variation #3:

• Striped ribbon with two or more ribbon streamers are hot-glued around crown of hat and a sprinkling of daisies is hot-glued onto front of ribbon and hat.

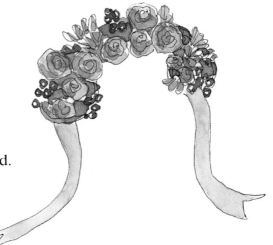

Variation #4 (straw hat not required):

• Silk flowers are glued onto the center of a 1½ yd. piece of ribbon.

Adorable
Furniture for the Parlor

Parlor Table

Materials:
Acrylic paints: cream; blue green; apple red; red violet
Crackle medium
Decal or greeting card picture
Découpage medium
Fabric glue
Gesso: white
Lace: 5"-wide, 1 yd.
Nontoxic varnish: gloss
Wooden doll table with pedestal leg: 12¾"w x 9¼"h x 12¾"l

Equipment:
Craft scissors
Paintbrushes:
    detail: #8
    flat: ½"; 1"
Pencil
Ruler

Instructions:

Step 1

a. See General Instructions for Paintbrushes on page 10. Paint table with gesso. Allow to dry.

b. Paint table with cream. Allow to dry.

Step 2

a. Measure and mark center of tabletop.

b. Beginning at mark, draw vertical lines the width of the ruler as shown in Illustration A. Repeat with horizontal lines, creating a checkerboard pattern.

Step 3

a. Paint every other square with blue green. *Note: It is not necessary to paint squares exactly within lines. Tip: Minimize mistakes by marking an "X" in squares to be painted. Allow to dry.*

b. Paint pedestal with apple red. Allow to dry.

c. Paint polka dots on pedestal with red violet. Allow to dry.

Illustration A

d. Paint base of table with blue green. Allow to dry.

Step 4

a. See General Instructions for Découpage on page 10. Découpage decal onto center of table. Allow to dry.

b. Paint table with crackle medium, following manufacturer's instructions. Allow to dry.

c. Paint varnish over crackle medium. Allow to dry.

Step 5

a. Hot-glue lace around edge of table.

Terra-cotta Flower Pot

Materials:
Moss
Scrap paper
Terra-cotta flowerpot:
   3"-dia.
Tiny flowers and buds:
   dried or silk

Equipment:
Hot-glue gun with
   glue sticks

Instructions:

Step 1

a. Scrunch up scrap paper and place in bottom of flowerpot, stopping 1" from rim.

Step 2

a. Hot-glue moss onto paper until covered.

b. Hot-glue individual flowers and buds onto moss until covered.

Fancy Wardrobe

Materials:
Acrylic paints: cream; lt. green
Art: color copies
Crackle medium (optional)
Découpage medium
Gesso: white
Nontoxic varnish: gloss
Wood glue
Wooden doll wardrobe:
    12"w x 20¼"h x 5⅜"l
Wooden trims:
    5⅜" x 1⅛" (1)
    corners: 3⅛" x 2⅜" (2)
    rosettes: 3"-dia. (2)

Equipment:
Clean soft rags
Craft scissors
Paintbrushes:
    detail: #6
    flat: ½"; 1"

Suitor at the Door Art

Illustration A

Instructions:

Step 1

a. Glue trims onto wardrobe as shown in Illustration A. Allow to dry.

Step 2

a. See General Instructions for Paintbrushes on page 10. Paint wardrobe with gesso. Allow to dry.

b. Paint wardrobe with lt. green.

Step 3

a. Color copy Suitor at the Door Art above and Mama Mouse Art on page 56. *Note: A favorite picture from a greeting card or children's book may be used in place of art.*

Mama Mouse Art

b. Cut out copied art.

c. See General Instructions for Découpage on page 10. Découpage one piece of art onto each upper panel of wardrobe door.

Step 4

a. Paint a small section of wardrobe with cream. Using soft rag, wipe off paint as shown in Illustration B. Repeat until wardrobe is antiqued as desired. Allow to dry.

b. *Optional: Paint wardrobe with crackle medium, following manufacturer's instructions. Allow to dry.*

c. Paint wardrobe with varnish. Allow to dry.

Illustration B

Tailored Chair Cover

Tailored Chair Cover

Materials:
Cording: 2 yd.
Fabrics:
    lining: ¼ yd.
    quilted: 1 yd.
Lace: 4"-wide (scrap)
Sewing thread
Wooden chair: painted,
    6¾"w x 15"h x 6¾"l

Equipment:
Fabric scissors
Sewing machine
    with zipper foot
Sewing needle
Straight pins
Tape measure

Instructions:

Step 1

a. Cut two 9½" x 11" rectangles from quilted fabric for chair back.

b. Cut one 7¾" x 8½" rectangle from quilted fabric for chair seat.

c. Measure widths of bottom front and back of chair and add 1" to each.

d. Using above measurements for width x 5", cut one piece each from quilted and lining fabrics for chair front and back drops.

e. Measure one side of chair and add 1".

f. Using above measurement for width x 5", cut two pieces each from lining and quilted fabrics for chair side drops.

g. Cut two 1½" x 36" strips for cording.

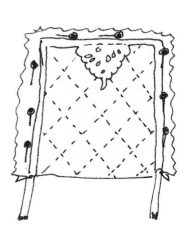

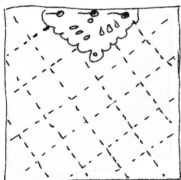

Illustration A

Step 2

a. Center lace scrap on right side of one quilted fabric piece for chair back as shown in Illustration A. *Note: Lace may also run across width of back.*

b. *Optional: See General Instructions for Cording on page 11. Make two pieces of finished cording by cutting cording in half and using 1½" strips of fabric.*

c. *Pin one piece of stitched cording around sides and top to right side of quilted chair back piece as shown in Illustration C.*

Illustration B

Illustration C

d. Using sewing machine, stitch sides and top of chair back pieces with right sides together and ½" seam allowance. Turn right side out.

e. Place chair back cover on chair and make any necessary adjustments.

Step 3

a. *Optional: Pin one piece of stitched cording around chair sides and front to right side of quilted chair seat piece as shown in Illustration C on page 59.*

b. Stitch raw edges of chair seat and chair back cover with right sides together as shown in Illustration D.

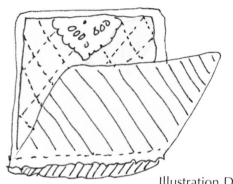

Illustration D

Step 4

a. Stitch sides and bottom of lining and quilted chair front drop pieces with right sides together. Turn right side out.

b. Repeat with remaining chair back and side drop pieces.

Step 5

a. Stitch chair front and side drop pieces to chair seat with quilted sides together as shown in Illustration E.

b. Stitch chair back drop piece to chair back cover.

c. Place chair seat cover on chair and make any necessary adjustments.

Illustration E

d. See General Instructions for Stitches on page 10. Using needle and thread, overcast-stitch 1"–1½" down from top of corners as shown in Illustration F. *Note: Edges may be tacked in place and trimmed with a ribbon bow.*

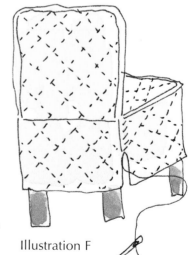

Illustration F

Whimsical Rocking Chair

Whimsical Rocking Chair

Materials:
Acrylic paints: lt. blue; lt. flesh; red violet
Fabric: ½ yd.
Fringe trim: 1"-wide, 1 yd.
Polyester stuffing
Rickrack: small (1 pkg.)
Sewing thread
Wooden cutouts:
    dolls: 7" (2)
    moon: 1½"
Wooden doll rocking chair:
    6¾"w x 15"h x 6¾"l

Equipment:
Fabric scissors
Hot-glue gun and glue sticks
Paintbrushes:
    detail: #6
    flat: 1"
Sewing machine

Illustration A

Instructions:

Step 1

a. See General Instructions for Paintbrushes on page 10. Paint chair and dolls with lt. blue. Allow to dry.

b. Paint front side of dolls' heads, hands, and feet with lt. flesh as shown in Illustration A. Allow to dry.

c. Paint moon and front side of dolls' dresses with red violet. Allow to dry.

Step 2

a. Hot-glue dolls onto back of chair as shown in photograph at right.

b. Hot-glue moon onto center of top rail.

c. Tie rickrack around dolls.

Step 3

a. Cut one 5" x 45" strip of fabric for chair ruffle.

b. Turn hem under ⅜" and stitch.

c. Stitch rickrack ½" above hem.

d. See General Instructions for Stitches on page 10. Gather-stitch double row around unhemmed edge and gather fabric.

e. Hot-glue gathered edge of ruffle around edge of seat.

f. Hot-glue fringe trim onto gathered edge of ruffle.

Step 4

a. Cut two 5½" squares for seat cushion.

b. Stitch three sides of rectangles with right sides together and ½" seam allowance. Turn right side out.

c. Lightly fill with stuffing. Fold ends in and stitch closed.

Adorable
Furniture for the Study

Floor Lamp

Materials:
Braid: 1"-wide, 28"
Chair leg turning: 19½"
Fringe trim: 2"-wide, 28" (optional)
Gesso: white
Lamp shade: 10"
Nontoxic varnish: turquoise gloss
Paintbrushes:
    flat: ½"; 1"
Screw: 3"
Sewing thread (optional)
Wood glue
Wooden ball knob: 1½"
Wooden circle: 8"-dia., 1"-thick (may
    be cut from scrap wood)

Equipment:
Drill with drill bits
Fabric scissors
Hot-glue gun and glue sticks
Screwdriver
Sewing needle (optional)

Instructions:

Step 1

a. Drill hole in center of circle for screw.

b. Attach turning to circle with screw as shown in Illustration A.

c. Using wood glue, glue knob onto top of turning for bulb. Allow to dry.

Illustration A

Step 2

a. See General Instructions for Paintbrushes on page 10. Paint lamp with gesso. Allow to dry.

b. Paint lamp with varnish. Allow to dry.

Step 3

a. Hot-glue braid around base of lamp as shown in Illustration B.

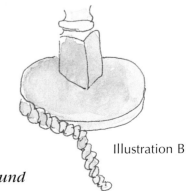

Illustration B

Step 4 (optional)

a. *Using needle and thread, stitch fringe around bottom edge of lamp shade.*

Floor Lamp

Wrapped & Ruffled Ribbon Lamp Shade

(Right lamp shade in photo)

Materials:
Lamp shade: 10"
Ribbon: 1⅜"-wide, wire-edged,
    sheer, 8 yds.

Equipment:
Fabric scissors
Hot-glue gun and glue sticks

Instructions:

Step 1

a. Fold one wire edge of ribbon under ¼".

b. Hot-glue folded edge of ribbon around top of shade.

c. Wrap and hot-glue ribbon around shade overlapping ribbon edges until entire shade is covered.

d. Trim off excess ribbon and hot-glue raw edge onto inside bottom of shade.

Braid and Ribbon Lamp Shade

(Left lamp shade in photo on page 67)

Materials:
Braiding: ½"-wide, 2 yds.
Fringe: ½"-wide, 1 yd.
Lamp shade: 10"
Ribbon: 1⅜"-wide, wire-edged,
    sheer, 8 yds.

Equipment:
Fabric scissors
Hot-glue gun and glue sticks
Tape measure

Instructions:

Step 1

a. Measure height of shade. Cut ribbon into pieces ½" longer than shade height.

b. Hot-glue one end of ribbon onto inside top of shade. Pull ribbon piece straight down and hot-glue onto inside bottom of shade.

c. Hot-glue ribbon around shade, overlapping ribbon to cover entire shade.

Gauze Lamp Shade

(Middle lamp shade in photo on page 67)

Materials:
Gauze: white, 42" x 9"
Lamp shade: 10"
Sewing thread

Equipment:
Hot-glue gun and glue sticks
Large bowl
Sewing needle
Black tea bags: (2)

Instructions:

Step 1

a. Pour four cups boiling water into large bowl and add tea bags. Steep tea bags for five minutes.

b. Remove tea bags and allow tea to cool.

c. Place gauze in tea until desired shade is reached.

d. Rinse gauze under cool running water.

e. Tightly twist gauze and allow to dry.

Step 2

a. Place short ends of gauze together and stitch with ¼" seam.

b. Fold one long edge of gauze under ¼" and stitch in place.

c. Fold remaining long edge under ½". See General Instructions for Stitches on page 10. Gather-stitch ¼" from fold.

d. Pull gather-stitch threads and fit to top of lamp shade. Knot thread ends to secure.

e. Hot-glue gathered edge of gauze onto top of lamp shade.

Overstuffed Chair

Overstuffed Chair

Chair Frame

Materials:
Cardboard
Cardboard box with flaps:
　　8"w x 4¾"h x 11¾"l
Duct tape
Empty toilet tissue rolls (2)
Quilt batting: high-loft, twin size
Sewing thread
Spray adhesive

Equipment:
Heavy-duty scissors or utility knife
Needle: large upholstery
Tape measure

Instructions:

Step 1

a. Push flaps to inside of box on one end. Securely tape flaps closed on opposite end.

b. Cut one 11¾" x 14¾" piece for back and two 8" x 9¼" pieces for arms from cardboard.

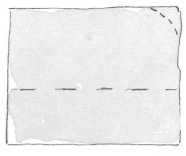
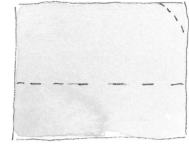

Illustration A

c. Trim and round one corner on arm pieces as shown in Illustration A.

d. Trim and round upper corners on back piece as shown in Illustration B.

Illustration B

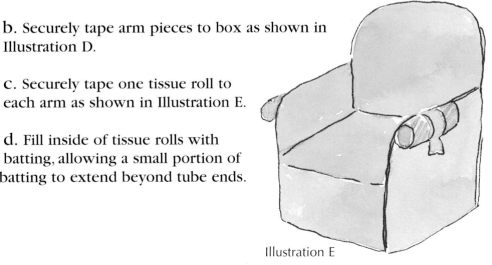

Illustration C

Step 2

a. Securely tape back to box as shown in Illustration C.

b. Securely tape arm pieces to box as shown in Illustration D.

c. Securely tape one tissue roll to each arm as shown in Illustration E.

d. Fill inside of tissue rolls with batting, allowing a small portion of batting to extend beyond tube ends.

Illustration D

Illustration E

71

Step 3

a. Enlarge Chair Cover Patterns 200% on pages
72-74 and photocopy. Cut out patterns.

Chair Cover Patterns

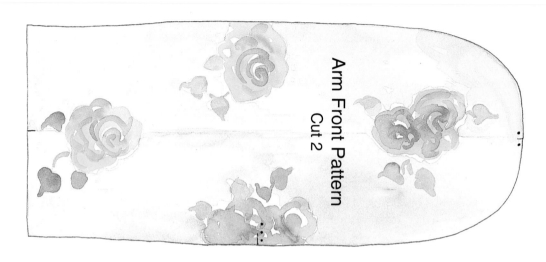

Arm Front Pattern
Cut 2

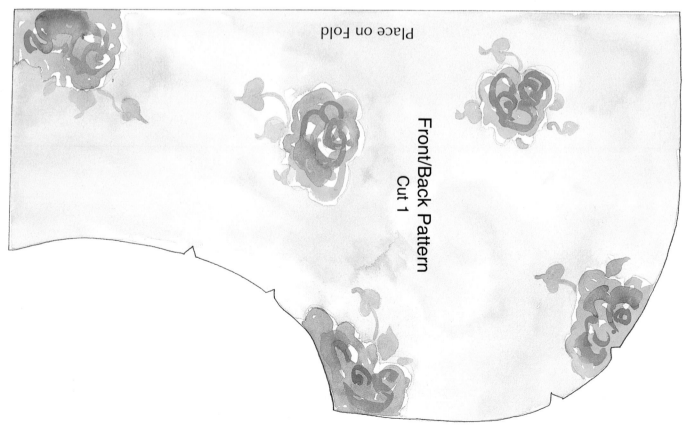

Place on Fold

Front/Back Pattern
Cut 1

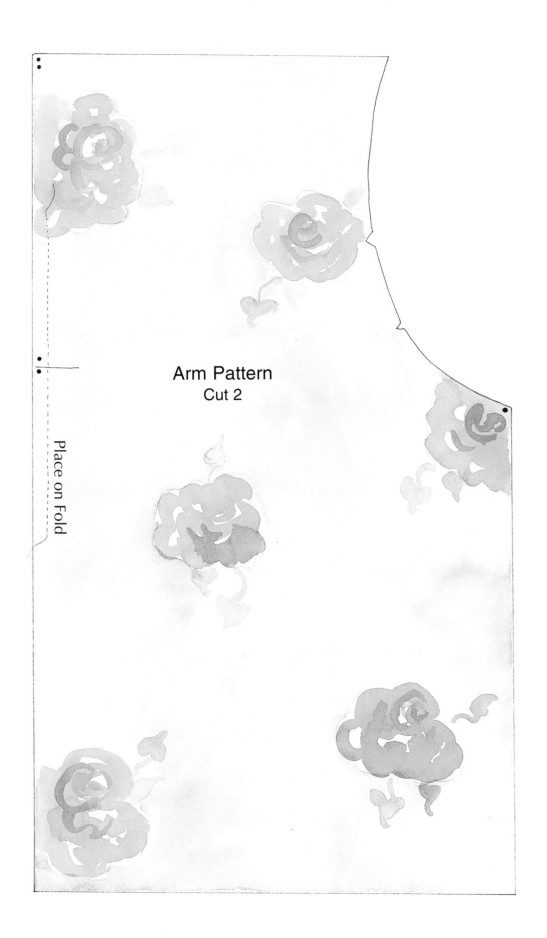

Arm Pattern
Cut 2

Place on Fold

Back Pattern
Cut 1

Place on Fold

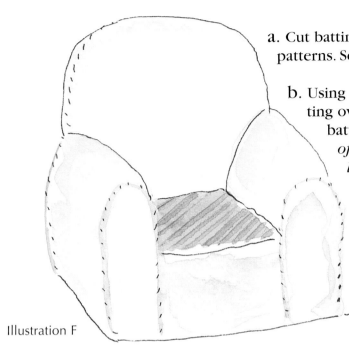

a. Cut batting double the lengths of the Arm and Front/Back patterns. Set patterns aside for Chair Slipcover instructions.

b. Using spray adhesive, spray one section and press batting over adhesive. Repeat for each section. Trim excess batting. *Note: If more loft is desired, a second piece of batting may be cut and applied over first layer of batting.*

c. See General Instructions for Stitches on page 10. Using needle and thread, stitch ends of arms and front together with large overcast stitch as shown in Illustration F. *Notes: Extra batting may be added to areas that may need more rounding. The slipcover will compress the batting when it is placed on chair.*

Illustration F

Chair Slipcover

Materials:
Braid: ½"-wide, 1½ yds.
Chair Cover Patterns
Fabric: cotton, 2½ yds.
Polyester stuffing
Sewing thread

Equipment:
Fabric marking pen
Fabric scissors
Hot-glue gun and glue sticks
Iron and ironing board
Masking tape
Pins:
    ball-head
    straight
    T-pins
Sewing machine
Sewing needle
Staple gun with staples
Tape measure

Instructions:

Step 1

a. Using straight pins, pin photocopied patterns from Overstuffed Chair Frame Steps 3 and 4a on pages 72 and 75 to fabric and cut out.

b. Cut one 11¼" x 13½" rectangle for seat/front of chair.

c. Cut three 5½" x 31" rectangles for chair ruffle.

d. Cut two 7½" x 11" rectangles for cushion.

e. Mark dots from patterns on right side of fabric.

Step 2

a. Drape chair Back and Front/Back pieces, right side up, over chair.

b. Match seams on inside. Using ball-head pins, pin pieces together for a snug fit as shown in Illustration G.

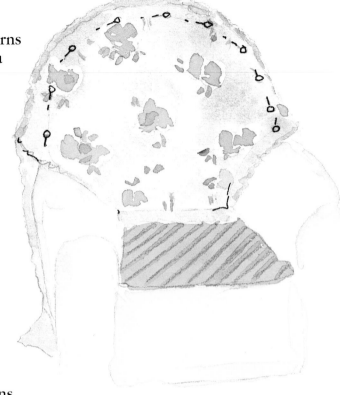

Illustration G

c. Trim excess fabric, leaving ¾" seam allowance. Cut notches every 2" to allow for curve and matching as shown in Illustration H. Remove cover from chair. Remove pins and place fabric with right sides together, matching notches. Using sewing machine, stitch pieces together.

d. Turn cover right side out and place on chair. Adjust any seams as necessary.

Illustration H

76

Step 3

a. Drape Arm piece over chair arm. Match dots on Arm piece to Front/Back piece. Pin inside arm seam together as shown in Illustration I.

b. Trim excess fabric, leaving ¾" seam allowance. Cut notches every 2" to allow for curve and matching.

c. Mark on fabric where stitching will begin and end. Remove cover from chair. Remove pins and place fabric with right sides together, matching notches. Stitch pieces together.

d. Stitch running stitch across top of arm as indicated on Arm Pattern.

Illustration I

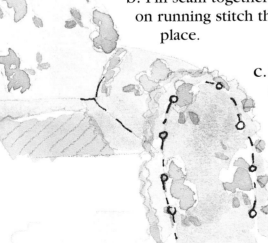

Step 4

a. Turn cover right side out and place on chair. Line up dots on Arm piece with dots on Arm Front piece.

b. Pin seam together as shown in Illustration J, pulling on running stitch thread to ease fabric curve in place.

c. Trim excess fabric, leaving ¾" seam allowance. Cut notches as necessary to allow for curve and matching.

d. Remove cover from chair. Remove pins and place fabric with right sides together, matching notches. Stitch pieces together.

Illustration J

Step 5

a. Place cover on chair and check fit. Add stuffing to fill out areas or make adjustments as needed.

b. Staple or tape raw fabric edges to box as shown in Illustration K.

Step 6

a. Fold under ½" on 13½" side of seat/front piece and press.

b. Place folded edge to back of seat. Fold side edges under to fit shape of seat.

c. Hot-glue seat section in place, allowing front edge to loosely hang down.

d. See General Instructions for Stitches on page 10. Using needle and thread, overcast-stitch arm and seat/front together.

e. Turn bottom raw edges of fabric inside box and hot-glue in place.

Illustration K

Step 7

a. Using sewing machine, stitch chair ruffle pieces together with ½" seam allowance to make one long strip.

b. Stitch ½" hem on one long side of ruffle.

c. Using sewing machine, gather-stitch two rows on long raw edge of ruffle. Gather ruffle to fit around chair.

d. Hot-glue gathered edge of ruffle around bottom edge of chair.

e. Hot-glue braid onto gathered edge of ruffle.

Step 8

a. Stitch three sides of cushion pieces with right sides together and ½" seam allowance. Turn right side out.

b. Fill cushion with stuffing. Fold ends in and stitch closed.

Alternate Instructions for Overstuffed Chair on pages 62–71:

Alternate Instructions:

Additional Materials:
Fabric: ½ yd.
Cording: 1 yd.

Additional Equipment:
Zipper foot

Step 1

a. Follow Chair Frame Instructions on pages 70–75.

Step 2

a. Follow Chair Slipcover Instructions on pages 75–78 through Step 7c.

b. See General Instructions for Cording on page 11. Cut 2" x 36" fabric strip for cording.

c. Stitch raw edge of cording to raw gathered edge of ruffle.

d. Hot-glue corded ruffle around bottom edge of chair.

e. Follow Chair Slipcover Instructions Step 8 for cushions.

Secretary

Materials:
Acrylic paints: metallic gold; green; lt. green
Decal or greeting card
Découpage medium
Gesso: white
Nontoxic varnish: gloss
Wood glue
Wooden trims:
    8" x 5" (1)
    5⅜" x 1" (1)
Wooden unfinished desk:
    10"w x 14¼"h x 7"l

Equipment:
Craft scissors
Measuring cup
Measuring spoons
Paintbrushes:
    detail: #6
    flat: ½"; 1"
Pencil

Instructions:

Step 1

a. Glue 8" x 5" trim to top edge of desk.

b. Glue 5⅜" x 1" trim onto front of desk.

Step 2

a. Mix ½ cup gesso with 1 tablespoon each of green and lt. green. Add additional paint in equal parts until desired color is reached. Mix well to completely blend colors.

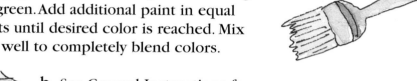

b. See General Instructions for Paintbrushes on page 10. Paint desk. Allow to dry.

c. Apply second coat of paint. Allow to dry.

Step 3

a. Cut out decal or greeting card art.

b. See General Instructions for Découpage on page 10. Découpage decal onto top of desk. Allow to dry.

c. Apply second coat of découpage medium. Allow to dry.

Step 4

a. Using pencil, lightly draw decorative designs.

b. Paint decorative designs over pencil marks with metallic gold. Allow to dry. Erase any pencil marks that may show.

c. Paint desk with varnish. Allow to dry.

Desk Chair Dress

Desk Chair Dress

Materials:
Fabric: plaid, ½ yd.
Wooden chair: painted,
   6¾"w x 15"h x 6¾"l

Equipment:
Fabric scissors
Sewing machine
Sewing needle
Straight pins
Tape measure

Instructions:

Step 1

a. Cut two 9" x 10½"
rectangles for chair back.

b. Cut one 7¼" x 8" rectangle for chair seat.

c. Cut one 6" x 44" strip for ruffle.

Step 2

a. Using sewing machine, stitch ½" hem on one long side of ruffle.

b. See General Instructions for Stitches on page 10. Using sewing machine, gather-stitch two rows on long raw edge of ruffle. Gather to fit around chair.

Step 3

a. Stitch three sides of chair back pieces with right sides together and ¼" seam allowance, leaving one 9" side open as shown in Illustration A.

b. Stitch seat to one raw edge of chair back with right sides together as shown in Illustration A.

c. Beginning at middle of seat, pin ruffle to seat with right sides together.

Illustration A

d. Stitch ruffle in place with ¼" seam allowance.

e. Turn chair back right side out and slip over chair.

Adorable
Furniture for the Dining Room

Romantic Hutch

Materials:
Acrylic paints: metallic gold; ivory
Découpage medium
Gesso: white
Greeting cards: botanical prints (2)
Nontoxic varnish: gloss
Wood glue
Wooden doll hutch:
    11"w x 20"h x 5½"l
Wooden trim:
    7⅞" x 4⅞"

Equipment:
Clothespins
Craft scissors
Paintbrushes:
    detail: #8
    flat: 1"

Instructions:

Step 1

a. Glue trim onto top of hutch as shown in Illustration A. Using clothespins, clamp in place. Allow to dry.

Step 2

a. See General Instructions for Paintbrushes on page 10. Paint hutch with gesso. Allow to dry.

b. Paint hutch with ivory. Allow to dry.

Illustration A

Step 3

a. Trim greeting card art to fit center square of doors.

b. See General Instructions for Découpage on page 10. Découpage art onto doors. Allow to dry.

Step 4

a. Outline edge of cards, edge of curves on front, drawer knobs, and highlight curves on trim with metallic gold. Allow to dry.

Step 5

a. Paint hutch with varnish. Allow to dry.

Lacy Shelf Liners

Materials:
Lace: scallop-edged

Equipment:
Fabric scissors
Hot-glue gun and glue sticks
Tape measure

Instructions:

Step 1

a. Measure width of shelves and cut lace to fit.

b. Hot-glue lace onto edge of shelves.

Découpage Frame

Materials:
Art: color copy
Craft glue
Découpage medium
Fabric: scrap
Masking tape
Picture mat with cardboard
    backing: 3" x 5"
Ribbon
Trim

Equipment:
Fabric scissors
Paintbrush:
    flat: 1"
Pencil

c. Glue top and bottom flaps onto back of frame. Allow to dry.

d. Glue inside triangles onto back of frame. Allow to dry. *Tip: Place duct tape over glued edges to hold fabric in place until dry.*

Step 3

a. Using craft glue, adhere ribbon and trim around frame opening.

Step 4

a. *Optional: Enlarge Little Mouse Art at left 112% and photocopy.*

b. Tape photocopy to back of frame.

c. Glue backing onto back of frame.

Instructions:

Step 1

a. Using paintbrush, apply découpage medium to front side of picture mat. Center and place right side of mat onto wrong side of fabric.

Tip: Decorative paper may be used in place of fabric, following Découpage instructions on page 10.

Step 2

a. Cut "X" from corner to corner of inside of frame as shown in Illustration A.

b. Glue side flaps onto back of frame. Allow to dry.

Illustration A

91

Acorn Chair & Table

Materials:
Acorns: (2)
Acrylic paints: crimson red;
    antique white
Breadboard with wooden legs: 9" x 9"
Decorator glaze: neutral
Mushroom bird: tiny
Sandpaper
Wood glue
Wooden curtain rod finials: (4)
Wooden doll chair: 5"w x 10"h x 5"l

Equipment:
Clean soft rags
Drill and drill bits
Hot-glue gun and glue sticks
Paintbrushes:
    flat: ½"; 1"
Pencil
Ruler
Sanding block (optional)
Sponge (optional)

Instructions:

Step 1

a. Drill hole in bottom center of each breadboard leg for finial screws.

b. Glue and screw finials to breadboard legs as shown in Illustration A. Allow to dry.

Illustration A

Step 2

a. See General Instructions for Paintbrushes on page 10. Paint table and chair with crimson red. Allow to dry.

Step 3

a. Measure and mark center of tabletop as shown in Illustration B.

b. Beginning at mark, draw vertical lines the width of the ruler as shown in Illustration C. Repeat with horizontal lines, creating a checkerboard pattern.

Illustration B

Illustration C

Step 4

a. Mix crimson red and antique white to desired shade. Paint every other square with mixture as shown in Illustration D. *Optional: Cut a sponge to desired size square and sponge-paint squares on table. Note: It is not necessary to paint squares exactly within lines.* Allow to dry overnight.

Illustration D

b. Paint seat of chair with crimson red and antique white mixture. Allow to dry.

c. Lightly sand all surfaces of table and chair. Using soft clean rag, wipe off dust from painted surface.

d. Paint table and chair with glaze. Using soft clean rag, wipe off excess. Allow to dry.

Step 5

a. Remove caps from acorns and hot-glue caps onto top of chair.

b. Hot-glue bird onto chair rail.

Braided Rug

Materials:
Jute cord
Sewing thread: heavy-duty
Wool fabric: (3 colors) *(may be recycled from old clothing)*

Equipment:
Braiders: (3)
Clamp
Fabric scissors
Needles:
    lacing *(bobby pin may be substituted)*
    sewing
Safety pins: large (3–4)
Sewing machine
Washing machine and dryer

Instructions:

Step 1

a. Wash wool in hot water and detergent. *Note: Wash colors separately since some colors may bleed.*

b. Dry wool in dryer.

Step 2

a. Cut or tear 1½" strips of wool along length of fabric. *Notes: Check braider's width and adjust strip width accordingly. Strips should be 12" or longer if recycled from clothing.*

Step 3

a. Using sewing machine, stitch strips of same color together on the bias. Trim seam.

b. Continue stitching strips together until a 6'–8' length is reached.

c. Repeat with remaining colors of wool.

Step 4

a. Square off ends of wool strips.

b. Slide rug braiders onto wool strips 12" from ends with wrong side down and folding under.

c. Using sewing needle and thread, stitch two strips together side-by-side around ends with edges under and knot.

d. Place third strip right side up under stitched strips, keeping edges folded in.

e. Stitch through the three strips and knot.

Step 5

a. Pull third strip back up over other strips so that right side is up. *Note: This places it in the center.*

b. Clamp stitched end of braid to table. *Note: Braid may be tied to a door knob or other stationary point if clamp is unavailable.*

c. Hold the braiders taut and begin braiding, maintaining a constant tension.

d. Remove braid and clamp in new position as braiding proceeds. *Note: Secure braid with safety pin when setting braid aside.*

e. Continue braiding until braid is approximately 45" long. *Note: Stitch additional wool strips to unbraided ends and continue braiding as needed.*

Step 6

a. Place safety pin through braid at 18" and 45".

b. Remove braid from clamp.

c. Fold braid in half at first safety pin.

d. Using lacing needle and jute cord, begin at end by sliding needle under inside section of braid.

e. Slide needle through inside section of braid on opposite section. Continue lacing braid together until bend is reached. *Note: Pull cord taut every few inches.*

f. Turn braid over and bring needle and cord back to surface.

g. Relace braid back toward end, going through opposite braid sections.

Step 7

a. Continue to lace braid together, stopping at 6". *Note: When coiling rug around curves, bring needle through three braids.*

b. Place braid in clamp and continue braiding, stopping to lace rug together. *Note: Attach additional cord with overhand knot, keeping cord one continuous piece.*

Step 8

a. When rug reaches desired size, secure with safety pin and remove braiders. *Note: Braid should end on a curve.*

b. Taper braided strips to a point beginning 12" from the end.

c. Continue lacing braid to rug until end is reached.

d. Wrap cording around end of braid and slide under braid on opposite side, pulling end into braid.

e. Wrap cord back around braid and secure end as invisibly as possible.

Egg and Tassels Chair

Materials:

Acrylic paints: black; turquoise

Laces:

½"-wide, 22"

5"-wide, 22"

Tassel trim: 1"-wide, gold, 1 yd.

Turquoise earring or

button: 1"

Wood glue

Wooden doll chair:

6¾"w x 15"h x 6¾"l

Wooden eggs: 3" (2)

Wooden medallion trim:

3" square

Equipment:

Hot-glue gun and glue sticks

Paintbrushes:

detail: #6

flat: ½"; 1"

Instructions:

Step 1

a. Using wood glue, glue medallion onto center of upper back slat as shown in Illustration A. Allow to dry.

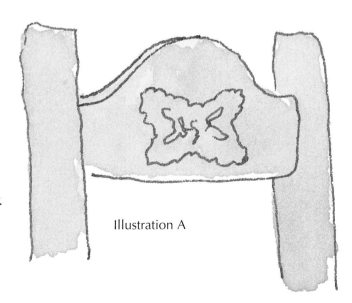

Illustration A

Step 2

a. See General Instructions for Paintbrushes on page 10. Paint eggs with turquoise. Allow to dry.

b. Paint chair with black. Allow to dry.

c. Hot-glue eggs onto top of chair.

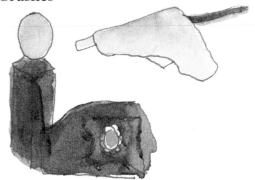

Step 3

a. Hot-glue 5"-wide lace around edge of seat, stopping at back rails.

b. Hot-glue tassel trim over 5"-wide lace.

c. Hot-glue tassel trim across bottom of top two back slats.

d. Hot-glue ½"-wide lace over tassel trim, around edge of seat.

e. Remove back from earring and hot-glue earring onto center of medallion.

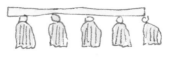

Adorable
Furniture for the Bedroom

Lacy Victorian Bed

Bed Frame

Materials:
Gesso: white
Nontoxic varnish: gloss
Wood glue
Wooden trims:
    12⅜" x 2¾" (1)
    5" x 2¾" (1)
    2" x 9¼" (2)
    3" x 3" (2)
Wooden unfinished doll bed:
    13"w x 21"h x 21"l

Equipment:
Paintbrushes:
    detail: #6; #8
    flat: ½"; 1"
Pencil
Straight pins
Tape measure

Instructions:

Step 1

a. Glue 12⅜" x 2¾" trim onto center of headboard and 3" x 3" trims onto headboard posts.

b. Glue 5" x 2¾" trim onto center of footboard and 2" x 9¼" trims onto footboard posts as shown in Illustration A.

Step 2

a. See General Instructions for Paintbrushes on page 10. Paint bed with gesso. Allow to dry.

b. Apply second coat of gesso. Allow to dry.

Step 3

a. Paint bed with varnish. Allow to dry.

b. Apply second coat of varnish. Allow to dry.

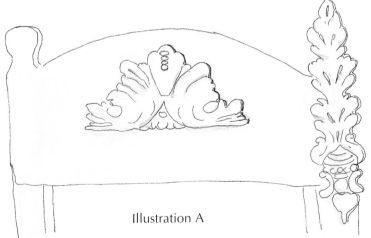

Illustration A

Bedding

Materials:
Fabric: ½ yd.; ⅓ yd.
Kitchen hand towel with decorative
    trim: cotton
Lace or flannel fabric: ½ yd.
Polyester stuffing
Sewing thread

Equipment:
Fabric scissors
Hot-glue gun and glue sticks
Sewing machine
Sewing needle
Tape measure

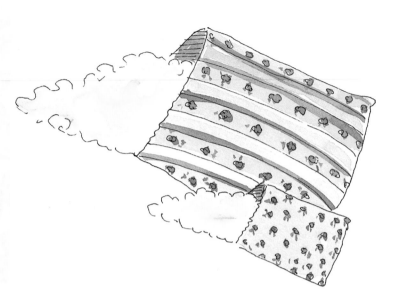

Instructions:

Step 1

a. Cut ⅓ yd. fabric into two 6" x 36" strips.

b. Using sewing machine, stitch 1" hem on one long side of each strip.

c. See General Instructions for Stitches on page 10. Using needle and thread, gather-stitch long raw edge of strips.

d. Hot-glue gathered edge of ruffle onto underside edge of bed.

Step 2

a. Measure inside width and length of bed. Cut two rectangles 1" larger than inside bed dimensions from ½ yd. fabric for mattress.

b. Using sewing machine, stitch three sides of rectangles with right sides together and ½" seam allowance. Turn right side out.

c. Lightly fill with stuffing. Fold ends in and stitch closed.

Step 3

a. Cut four rectangles half the width of the bed plus 1" x 4" from ½ yd. fabric for pillows.

b. Stitch three sides of two rectangles with right sides together and ½" seam allowance. Turn right side out.

c. Follow instructions for Step 2c.

d. Repeat for second pillow.

Step 4

a. Using same dimensions for pillows plus ½", cut four rectangles from hand towel, placing decorative trim on one short side for pillowcases.

b. Stitch two rectangles on three sides with right sides together, allowing decorative edge to remain unstitched. Turn right side out. Repeat for remaining pillowcase.

Step 5

a. Cut lace or flannel fabric large enough to hem and tuck under mattress for blanket.

104

Lace & Rose Pillow

Materials:
Lace-edged scarf or dresser scarf:
    approx. 7" x 8"
Polyester stuffing
Ribbon: ¾"-wide, 1 yd.
Sewing thread
Silk Roses

Equipment:
Fabric scissors
Hot-glue gun and glue sticks (optional)
Sewing needle

Instructions:

Step 1

a. Fold scarf in half lengthwise with right sides together.

b. Stitch long edges together and turn right side out.

c. Lightly fill center with stuffing.

Step 2

a. Cut ribbon in half.

b. Tie ribbon around open ends of tube as shown in Illustration A.

Illustration A

Step 3

a. Hot-glue or tuck silk roses under ribbon.

Variations

• Stitch lace around the edge and a pretty lace medallion in the center of cotton or fine net.

• A lace table scarf or runner can be used by cutting excess fabric from center and stitching back together.

• An antique dresser scarf makes a beautiful vintage-style pillow.

Pillow Chair

Materials:
Braid: ½"-wide, 1½ yd.
Cardboard: 10" x 10"
Fabrics: cotton prints, ⅓ yd.; 1 yd.
Polyester stuffing
Threads:
    carpet
    sewing

Equipment:
Carpet needle
Fabric scissors
Hot-glue gun and glue sticks
Sewing machine
Straight pins
Tape measure

Instructions:

Step 1

a. Cut two 11" squares from 1 yd. fabric for seat.

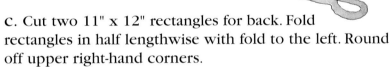

b. Cut four 6½" x 11" rectangles for arms.

c. Cut two 11" x 12" rectangles for back. Fold rectangles in half lengthwise with fold to the left. Round off upper right-hand corners.

Step 2

a. Using sewing machine, place seat pieces with right sides together and stitch on three sides with ½" seam allowance.

b. Slide cardboard into open end.

c. Fill open end with stuffing on one side of cardboard. Fold ends in and stitch closed.

d. Repeat Steps 2a and 2c for arm pieces and back pieces. *Note: One 11" side should be the unstitched side.*

Step 3

a. See General Instructions for Stitches on page 10. Using carpet needle and carpet thread, overcast-stitch 11" edges together as shown in Illustration A.

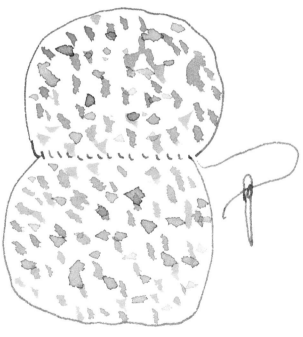

Illustration A

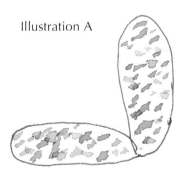

107

b. Overcast-stitch 11" edges of arms to seat, making certain that stuffed side of seat is up.

c. Overcast-stitch arms to back as shown in Illustration B.

Step 4

a. Cut two 5" x 44" strips for ruffle from ⅓ yd. fabric.

b. Using sewing machine, stitch short ends of strips together.

c. Trim strip to 54".

d. Stitch ½" hem on one long side of strip.

e. Gather-stitch two rows on long raw edge of strip. Gather ruffle to fit around chair.

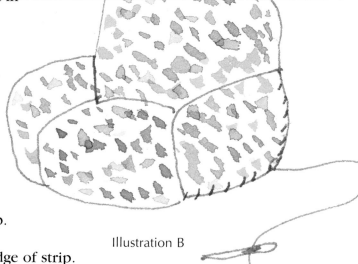

Illustration B

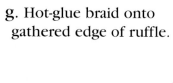

f. Hot-glue gathered edge of ruffle around bottom of chair.

g. Hot-glue braid onto gathered edge of ruffle.

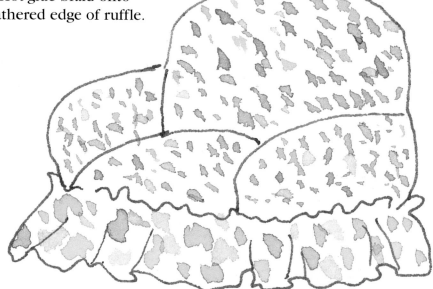

Candlestick End Table

Materials:
Bound book:
 approx. 4½" square
Crystal candleholder:
 3" tall

Equipment:
Hot-glue gun and
 glue sticks

Instructions:

Step 1
a. Hot-glue book onto top of candleholder.

Bed of Roses

Bed Frame

Materials:
Acrylic paint: lt. green (2)
Lace: 4"-wide, 1½ yds.
Rose garland
Wood glue
Wooden doll bed: 13"w x 21"h x 21"l
Wooden picket fences: 10" x 13" (2)

Equipment:
Hot-glue gun and glue sticks
Paintbrush:
    flat: 2"

Instructions:

Illustration A

Step 1

a. Using wood glue, adhere one picket fence onto outside of footboard as shown in Illustration A. Allow to dry.

b. Adhere one picket fence onto inside of headboard as shown in Illustration B. Allow to dry.

Step 2

a. Paint bed with green. Allow to dry.

b. Apply second coat of paint. Allow to dry.

Step 3

a. Hot-glue lace onto sides of bed.

b. Entwine rose garland around picket fences.

Illustration B

Bedding

Materials:
Fabric: ½ yd.; scraps
Lace fabric
Quilt batting: crib size

Equipment:
Fabric scissors
Sewing machine
Tape measure

Instructions:

Step 1

a. Measure inside of bed. Cut two rectangles from fabric, using these dimensions plus 1" for mattress.

b. Using sewing machine, stitch three sides of rectangles with right sides together and ½" seam allowance. Turn right side out.

c. Cut 2–3 layers of batting, using inside bed dimensions.

d. Slide batting into mattress cover. Fold ends in and stitch closed.

Step 2

a. Cut four rectangles that are half the width of the bed plus 1" x 4" from fabric scraps for pillows.

b. Stitch three sides of two rectangles with right sides together and ½" seam allowance. Turn right side out.

c. Lightly fill with batting. Fold ends in and stitch closed.

d. Repeat for second pillow.

Step 3

a. Cut lace large enough to hem for bed covering.

Variations

- Substitute fringe for lace around edge of bed.

- Place baby's breath flowers around head-board and drape a tassel over footboard in place of rose garland.

Mouse's Bed

Mouse's Bed

Bed Frame

Materials:
Acrylic paint: sky blue
Gesso: white
Nontoxic varnish: gloss
Wood glue
Wooden mason jars: ¾" x ¹⁵⁄₁₆" (4)
Wooden serving tray or box:
    12¾"w x 4½"h x 10"l
Wooden trims:
    10½" x 2½" (1)
    1¾" x 9¼" (1)

Equipment:
Paintbrushes:
    detail: #6
    flat: ½"; 1"
Pencil

Mattress

Materials:
Fabric: striped, ⅓ yd.
Polyester stuffing
Sewing thread

Equipment:
Fabric scissors
Sewing machine
Tape measure

Instructions:

Step 1

a. Glue 10½" x 2½" trim onto inside of one end of tray for headboard.

b. Glue 1¾" x 9¼" trim onto outside of opposite end for footboard. Allow to dry.

c. Turn bed upside down and glue bottom end of mason jars onto corners for legs.

Step 2

a. See General Instructions for Paintbrushes on page 10. Paint bed with gesso. Allow to dry.

b. Paint bed with sky blue. Allow to dry.

c. Paint bed with varnish. Allow to dry.

Instructions:

Step 1

a. Measure inside dimensions of bed.

b. Cut two rectangles 1" larger than bed dimensions.

c. Stitch three sides of rectangles with right sides together and ½" seam allowance.

d. Lightly fill with stuffing. Fold ends in and stitch closed.

Note: Pillows and pillowcases may be made, following Lacy Victorian Bed instructions for Bedding Step 3 and Step 4 on page 104.

Country Plaid Bed

Country Plaid Bed

Bed Frame

Materials:

Acrylic paints: olive green;
   apple red; dk. violet
Gesso: white
Nontoxic varnish: gloss
Wooden curtain rod finials: (4)
Wooden doll bed:
   18"w x 12"h x 22"l
Wooden trims:
   8" x 5"
   5¼" x 1"

Equipment:

Drill and drill bit
Paintbrushes:
   detail: #6
   flat: 1"
Sewing machine

Instructions:

Step 1

a. Glue 8" x 5" trim onto upper center of headboard. Allow to dry.

b. Glue 5½" x 1" trim onto center of footboard. Allow to dry.

Step 2

a. Drill hole in top of bed posts. Screw finials into bed posts.

Step 3

a. See General Instructions for Paintbrushes on page 10. Paint bed with gesso. Allow to dry.

b. Paint bottom frame around bed and bottom ring of finials with olive green. Allow to dry.

c. Paint legs and top of curtain finials with dk. violet. Allow to dry.

d. Paint headboard, footboard, sideboards, unpainted portions of

finials, and inside of bed with apple red. Allow to dry.

e. Paint dots with dk. violet on upper red portion of finials.

f. Paint stripes on sides of bed with dk. violet.

g. Paint bed with varnish. Allow to dry.

Bedding

Materials:
Cotton fabrics:
    gingham: ⅓ yd.
    print: 1 yd.
Polyester stuffing
Sewing thread

Equipment:
Fabric scissors
Sewing machine
Staple gun with staples
Tape measure

Instructions:

Step 1

a. Measure around bottom of bed and double measurement. Measure from ground to bottom of bed and add 1".

b. Cut strip from print fabric, using dimensions in Step 1a

for ruffle. *Note: If necessary, fabric may be cut into two or more strips and seamed together.*

c. Stitch ½" hem on one long side of strip.

d. See General Instructions for Stitches on page 10. Using sewing machine, gather-stitch two rows on long raw edge of ruffle. Gather ruffle to fit around bed. *Note: Ready-made ruffles may be purchased at a fabric store.*

e. Using staple gun, staple gathered edge of ruffle to underside of bed.

Step 2

a. Measure inside of bed. Cut two rectangles from gingham fabric, using these dimensions plus 1" for mattress.

b. Stitch three sides of rectangles with right sides together and ½" seam allowance. Turn right side out.

c. Lightly fill with stuffing. Fold ends in and stitch closed.

d. See Lacy Victorian Bed instructions for Bedding Step 3 and Step 4 on page 104 to make pillows and pillowcases. *Notes: An old quilt can be cut and bound to fit bed. Large handkerchiefs and decorative-edged cotton hand towels may be used for making pillowcases.*

Checkerboard Quilt

Materials:
Cotton fabrics:
    backing: ⅔ yd.
    red print: ⅓ yd.
    white: ¾ yd.
Quilt batting: low-loft, crib size
Threads:
    quilting
    sewing

Equipment:
Fabric marker: water-soluble (optional)
Fabric scissors
Iron and ironing board
Needles:
    quilting
    sewing
Pins
Quilting template (optional)
Sewing machine
Tape measure

Instructions:

Step 1

a. Cut twenty-four 2½" squares each from white and red print fabrics.
Notes: More or less squares may be cut, based on your doll bed size. Approximate finished size of quilt is 20" x 24".

b. Tear or cut four 4" x 24" strips for border from white fabric.

c. Cut four 1" x 24" bias strips for binding edge.

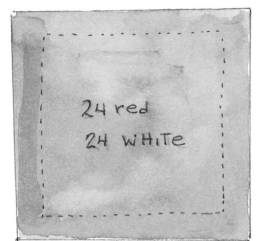

24 red
24 WHiTe

Step 2

a. Using sewing machine and alternating colors, stitch six squares together with ¼" seam allowance to make one row. Repeat with remaining squares until all are used. *Note: Press seams open after stitching.*

b. Alternating colors of rows, stitch rows together.

Step 3

a. Stitch borders to top and bottom of stitched rows. Trim off excess fabric.

b. Stitch remaining border strips to sides of stitched rows and borders. Trim off excess fabric.

Step 4

a. Cut backing and quilt batting to same dimensions as quilt top.

Step 5

a. Place batting between quilt top and backing and pin in place.

b. Using sewing needle and sewing thread, baste together.

Step 6

a. Using quilting needle and quilting thread, quilt around squares. *Note: Quilting may be done using sewing machine.*

b. *Optional: Using quilt template and fabric marker, draw scallops in wide border, then quilt.*

c. Quilt 1" rows around borders. *Note: Eliminate this if you follow 6b for quilting.*

Step 7

a. Place binding strips with right sides together on top and bottom edges of quilt top and pin in place.

b. Using sewing machine, stitch binding strips to quilt top and trim excess fabric.

c. Stitch binding strips to sides of quilt top and trim excess fabric.

Step 8

a. Fold binding over edge of quilt.

b. Turn raw edge under ¼" and using sewing needle and sewing thread, stitch to backing.

Log Cabin Quilt

Materials:

Cotton fabrics:
 backing: ⅔ yd.
 border print: ¼ yd.
 contrast print: ⅓ yd.
 dk. prints: ½ yd. (3)
 lt. prints: ½ yd. (2)
Threads:
 quilting
 sewing
Quilt batting: low-loft, crib size

Equipment:

Iron and ironing board
Fabric marker: water-soluble
Fabric scissors
Quilting template (optional)
Sewing machine

Instructions:

Step 1

a. Cut thirty 1½" squares from one dk. color. *Note: Approximate finished size of quilt is 20" x 23".*

b. Tear or cut dk. and lt. prints into 1" strips.

c. Tear or cut four 1½" x 24" and four 3" x 26" strips from border print.

d. Cut four 1" x 26" bias strips from border print for binding edge.

e. Tear or cut 1½" x 24" strip from contrast print.

Step 2

Assembling quilt blocks:

a. Using sewing machine, stitch one lt. print strip to top of fabric square with ¼" seam allowance. Trim off excess fabric. *Note: Press seams open after stitching.*

b. Stitch one lt. print strip to right side of quilt block. Trim off excess fabric.

c. Stitch one dk. print strip to bottom of quilt block. Trim off excess fabric.

d. Stitch one dk. print strip to left side of quilt block. Trim off excess fabric.

e. Repeat Steps 2a–b with second lt. print.

f. Repeat Steps 2c–d with second dk. print.

g. Repeat Steps 2a–f for remaining quilt blocks.

Step 3

a. Stitch five blocks together with light side of each block to right and bottom.

b. Stitch rows of quilt blocks together, matching lt. print to lt. print and dk. print to dk. print.

Step 4

a. Stitch 1½" border strip to top and bottom of rows. Trim off excess fabric.

b. Stitch remaining 1½" border strips to sides of stitched rows and borders. Trim off excess fabric.

c. Stitch 1½" contrast print strip to top and bottom of quilt. Trim off excess fabric.

d. Stitch remaining 1½" contrast print strip to sides of quilt. Trim off excess fabric.

e. Stitch 3" border strip to top and bottom of quilt. Trim off excess fabric.

f. Stitch remaining 3" border strips to sides of quilt. Trim off excess fabric.

Step 5

a. Cut backing and quilt batting to same dimensions as quilt top.

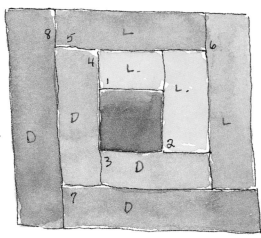

Illustration A

Step 6

a. Place batting between quilt top and backing, and pin in place.

b. Using sewing needle and sewing thread, baste together.

Step 7

a. Using quilting needle and quilting thread, quilt around squares. *Note: Quilting may be done using sewing machine.*

b. Quilt between border strips.

c. *Optional: Using quilt template and fabric marker, draw scallops in wide border of quilt.*

d. Quilt 1" rows around borders. *Note: Eliminate this step if you follow 7c for quilting.*

Step 8

a. Place binding strips with right sides down on top and bottom edges of quilt top and pin in place.

b. Using sewing machine, stitch binding strips to quilt. Trim off excess fabric.

c. Stitch binding strips to sides of quilt top. Trim off excess fabric.

Step 9

a. Fold binding over edge of quilt.

b. Turn raw edge under ¼" and using sewing needle and sewing thread, stitch to backing.

Scandinavian Painted Bed

Materials:
Acrylic paints: brown; cream; red
Antiquing medium
Gesso: white
Masking tape
Nontoxic varnish: gloss
Transfer paper
Wooden doll bed:
    13"w x 21"h x 21"l

Equipment:
Clean cotton rag
Paintbrushes:
    detail: #6
    flat: 1"
Pencil

Instructions:

Step 1

a. See General Instructions for Paintbrushes on page 10. Paint bed with gesso. Allow to dry.

b. Paint bed with cream. Allow to dry.

Step 2

a. Photocopy Headboard/Footboard Design and Left and Right Side Rail Designs.

b. Tape Headboard/Footboard Design over transfer paper and transfer design onto bed.

c. Tape Left and Right Side Rail Designs over transfer paper and transfer designs onto sides of bed.

d. Paint design onto bed with brown and red paint. Allow to dry. Paint any additional designs as desired.

Step 3

a. Outline shape of headboard and footboard with brown. Allow to dry.

Step 4

a. Paint antiquing medium onto bed in a small area and wipe off.

b. Continue to apply and wipe off antiquing medium over entire bed. Allow to dry overnight.

Step 5

a. Paint bed with varnish. Allow to dry.

Left Side Rail Design

When you are all done, don't forget to clean up!
The End

Metric Equivalency Chart

mm-millimetres   cm-centimetres
inches to millimetres and centimetres

inches	mm	cm	inches	cm	inches	cm
⅛	3	0.3	9	22.9	30	76.2
¼	6	0.6	10	25.4	31	78.7
⅜	10	1.0	11	27.9	32	81.3
½	13	1.3	12	30.5	33	83.8
⅝	16	1.6	13	33.0	34	86.4
¾	19	1.9	14	35.6	35	88.9
⅞	22	2.2	15	38.1	36	91.4
1	25	2.5	16	40.6	37	94.0
1¼	32	3.2	17	43.2	38	96.5
1½	38	3.8	18	45.7	39	99.1
1¾	44	4.4	19	48.3	40	101.6
2	51	5.1	20	50.8	41	104.1
2½	64	6.4	21	53.3	42	106.7
3	76	7.6	22	55.9	43	109.2
3½	89	8.9	23	58.4	44	111.8
4	102	10.2	24	61.0	45	114.3
4½	114	11.4	25	63.5	46	116.8
5	127	12.7	26	66.0	47	119.4
6	152	15.2	27	68.6	48	121.9
7	178	17.8	28	71.1	49	124.5
8	203	20.3	29	73.7	50	127.0

yards to metres

yards	metres	yards	metres	yards	metres	yards	metres	yards	metres
⅛	0.11	2⅛	1.94	4⅛	3.77	6⅛	5.60	8⅛	7.43
¼	0.23	2¼	2.06	4¼	3.89	6¼	5.72	8¼	7.54
⅜	0.34	2⅜	2.17	4⅜	4.00	6⅜	5.83	8⅜	7.66
½	0.46	2½	2.29	4½	4.11	6½	5.94	8½	7.77
⅝	0.57	2⅝	2.40	4⅝	4.23	6⅝	6.06	8⅝	7.89
¾	0.69	2¾	2.51	4¾	4.34	6¾	6.17	8¾	8.00
⅞	0.80	2⅞	2.63	4⅞	4.46	6⅞	6.29	8⅞	8.12
1	0.91	3	2.74	5	4.57	7	6.40	9	8.23
1⅛	1.03	3⅛	2.86	5⅛	4.69	7⅛	6.52	9⅛	8.34
1¼	1.14	3¼	2.97	5¼	4.80	7¼	6.63	9¼	8.46
1⅜	1.26	3⅜	3.09	5⅜	4.91	7⅜	6.74	9⅜	8.57
1½	1.37	3½	3.20	5½	5.03	7½	6.86	9½	8.69
1⅝	1.49	3⅝	3.31	5⅝	5.14	7⅝	6.97	9⅝	8.80
1¾	1.60	3¾	3.43	5¾	5.26	7¾	7.09	9¾	8.92
1⅞	1.71	3⅞	3.54	5⅞	5.37	7⅞	7.20	9⅞	9.03
2	1.83	4	3.66	6	5.49	8	7.32	10	9.14

Index